Canada Close Up

British Columbia

Carrie Gleason

Scholastic Canada Ltd.
Toronto New York London Auckland Sydney
Mexico City New Delhi Hong Kong Buenos Aires

Visual Credits

Cover: Roy Ooms/Masterfile; p. I: Chris Tripodi/ChrisTrip Photos; p. III: David R. Frazier Photolibrary, Inc./Alamy; p. IV: (top right) aceshot1/Shutterstock Inc., (middle left) Shutterstock Inc.; (middle right) iStockPhoto.com; p. 2: Josh McCulloch/Alamy; p. 3: (top) Chris Tripodi/ChrisTrip Photos, (bottom) Sam Abell/National Geographic Stock; p. 4: (top) Steven J. Kazlowski/Alamy; p. 5: (top) iStockPhoto.com, (bottom) Gunter Marx/Alamy; p. 6: © Canada Post Corporation {1990}. Reproduced with Permission; p. 7: Dietrich Rose/zefa/Corbis; p. 8: Thomas Kitchin & Victoria Hurst; p. 9: (top right and bottom) iStockPhoto.com; p. 10: Wave/First Light; p. 11: Russ Heinl/ AllCanadaPhotos.com; p. 12: Glenbow Archives; p. 13: The Granger Collection, New York; p. 14: (top) Glenbow Archives, (bottom) © Canada Post Corporation {1957}. Reproduced with Permission; p. 15: Image B-01549 courtesy of Royal BC Museum, BC Archives; p. 16: Glenbow Archives; p. 17: (top) iStockPhoto.com, (bottom) Glenbow Archives; p. 19: Glenbow Archives; p. 20: Image A-03255 courtesy of Royal BC Museum, BC Archives; p. 21: Glenbow Archives; p. 22: Tak Toyota/Library and Archives Canada/C-046350; p. 23: John Peter Photography/Alamy; p. 24: Randy Lincks/AllCanadaPhotos.com; p. 25: Josh McCulloch/AllCanadaPhotos.com; p. 26: Chris Cheadle/AllCanadaPhotos.com; p. 27: (top) iStockPhoto.com, (bottom) Chris Tripodi/ChrisTrip Photos; p. 28 and back cover: Gunter Marx/Alamy; p. 29: (bottom) onurdongel/iStockPhoto.com; p. 30: Chris Tripodi/ChrisTrip Photos; p. 31: (top) Watts/ Hall Inc/First Light, (bottom) Barrett & MacKay/AllCanadaPhotos.com; p. 32: (top) Chris Tripodi/ ChrisTrip Photos, (bottom) Chris Cheadle/AllCanadaPhotos.com; p. 33: (bottom) Radius Images/ AllCanadaPhotos.com; p. 34: (top) Joel W. Rogers/Corbis, (bottom) Gunter Marx/Alamy; p. 35: iStockPhoto.com; p. 36: Chris Tripodi/ChrisTrip Photos; p. 37: Chris Tripodi/ChrisTrip Photos; p. 38: Chris Cheadle/AllCanadaPhotos.com; p. 39: (top) Andre Jenny/Alamy, (bottom) Image E-04017 courtesty of Royal BC Museum, BC Archives; p. 40: Gunter Marx Photography/Corbis; p. 41: (top) Image B-00877 courtesy of Royal BC Museum, BC Archives, (bottom) Emily Carr, Heina, 1928. Photo © National Gallery of Canada, National Gallery of Canada, Ottawa; p. 42: (top) Douglas Lander/Alamy, (middle) CP Photo, (bottom left) AP Photo/Dita Alangkara; p. 43: (top) CP PHOTO/Jonathan Hayward, (bottom) CP PHOTO/Dick Green.

Produced by Plan B Book Packagers
Editorial: Ellen Rodger
Design: Rosie Gowsell-Pattison
Special thanks to consultant and editor Terrance Cox, adjunct professor, Brock University;
Adrianna Morganelli, Tanya Rutledge, Jim Chernishenko

Library and Archives Canada Cataloguing in Publication

Gleason, Carrie, 1973-
British Columbia / Carrie Gleason.
(Canada close up)
Includes index.
ISBN 978-0-545-98900-8

1. British Columbia--Juvenile literature. I. Title. II. Series: Canada
close up (Toronto, Ont.)
FC3811.2.G54 2009   j971.1   C2009-901198-0

ISBN-10 0-545-98900-0

6 5 4 3 2 1   Printed in Canada   09 10 11 12 13 14

Contents

The white blossoms of the Pacific dogwood are British Columbia's floral emblem.

The provincial bird is the Steller's jay.

Jade is the provincial gemstone.

CANADA

Russia

ARCTIC OCEAN

Greenland (Denmark)

Iceland

Alaska (U.S.A.)

Yukon

ATLANTIC OCEAN

Northwest Territories

Nunavut

Newfoundland and Labrador

PACIFIC OCEAN

British Columbia

Hudson Bay

Alberta

Saskatchewan

Manitoba

James Bay

Prince Edward Island

Ontario

Quebec

Nova Scotia

Lake Huron

New Brunswick

United States

Lake Superior

Lake Ontario

Lake Michigan

Lake Erie

Welcome to British Columbia!

From backyard slugs to giant western cedars and towering mountain ranges, there's one word to describe British Columbia – big. Although not the largest province in land size or population, B.C. has the most mountains, Canada's only rainforests and true desert, and rare animals like the spirit bear, found nowhere else on Earth.

The giant totem poles of the Northwest Coast must have amazed the area's first explorers. Today, they remind us how important B.C.'s cultural history and natural resources are to its past, present and future.

You can travel by plane over the Rocky Mountains, on a train through tunnels and up steep, **perilous** mountain tracks, or by boat along the Pacific coast. Come "out west" to beautiful B.C.!

Chapter 1
The Lay of the Land

British Columbia is as far west as you can go in Canada. The province's mainland lies between the Canadian Rockies and the Pacific Ocean. Thousands of islands off the coast also belong to it.

The Pacific province

British Columbia has over 27,000 kilometres of ocean coastline, including the shores of its 6500 islands. It's easy to see why its nickname is "the Pacific province."

Some of the islands are tiny and **uninhabited**. But Vancouver Island is large: 460 kilometres long. Its west side is wet, wild and rugged. The wind and pounding surf of the Pacific give shape to its many **fjords** and sounds.

Pacific Rim National Park, the island's only national park, is found along this coast. It features long sandy beaches, old-growth **temperate** rainforests and an **archipelago** of over 100 islands. Pods of orcas, sea lions, sea otters and harbour seals swim in the surrounding water.

B.C. has many ocean beaches.

Vancouver Island's east coast is covered in gentle hills and has mild, sunny weather. Lying off this coast, in the Strait of Georgia, is an archipelago of over 200 islands called the Gulf Islands.

Gulls and cormorants soar above basking sea lions along B.C.'s rocky coast.

Haida Gwaii

The Queen Charlotte Islands, also known as Haida Gwaii, is a chain of more than 150 islands north of Vancouver Island. The two largest islands are Graham Island and Moresby Island. They are part of the Great Bear Rainforest which extends along the central and north coast of B.C.

Kermode bears, also known as "spirit bears," are black bears with white fur. They live only in the B.C. rainforest.

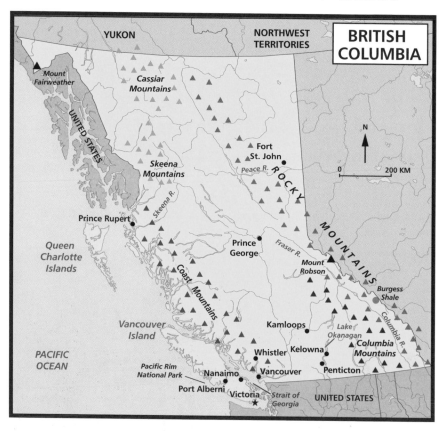

B.C.'s rainforests

One-quarter of the world's temperate rainforests are in British Columbia – along the coast, on the islands and on the mainland.

Banana slug

These forests grow where there is plenty of rainfall and mild temperatures. They are home to a wide range of plants such as mosses, lichen, ferns and fungi, and birds, insects and animals such as cougars, lynx, wolves, bears, deer and elk. Slick banana slugs, 15 to 20 centimetres long, slime their way across the forest floor.

The biggest trees in Canada are found in old-growth, or ancient, forests. Old-growth forests have never been cut down. Some trees are 1000 years old.

The Carmanah Giant, a Sitka spruce 95 metres tall, is Canada's tallest tree. It is found on the southwest coast of Vancouver Island.

5

The Coast Mountains

Most of British Columbia lies in Canada's Cordilleran Region, an area of mountain ranges, valleys, plateaus and plains. B.C.'s westernmost mountains are the Coast Mountains. They run along the Pacific coast and end at the lower mainland.

Valleys and lake monsters

In the mainland interior are low mountain ranges and plateaus. The climate here is much drier than on the coasts because the Coast Mountains block the wet winds that blow in from the Pacific Ocean.

In the southeast interior is the Okanagan Valley. This region is flat and the soil is fertile for growing crops. In the centre of the valley is Okanagan Lake. To the south is desert. Cacti, sagebrush, horned lizards, rattlesnakes and burrowing owls live in the dry, warm climate here.

According to legend, Okanagan Lake is home to a snake-like monster known as Ogopogo.

CANADA 3/9

THE OGOPOGO
L'OGOPOGO

More mountains

The Columbia Mountains include the Purcell, Selkirk, Monashee and Cariboo ranges. They are located in the southeast and are between 1800 and 3300 metres tall.

Separating the Columbia Mountains from the Rockies is the Rocky Mountain Trench. It is the longest valley in North America and a natural transportation route through the mountains. Huge peaks flank either side.

Although three-quarters of British Columbia is covered in mountains, none are as famous as the Rocky Mountains. This mountain chain extends all the way from northern B.C. to New Mexico in the United States. In Canada, the Rockies stretch 1360 kilometres along the B.C.-Alberta border. Mount Robson is the highest peak in the Canadian Rockies, at 3954 metres.

The Burgess Shale

The Burgess Shale is a strange place to study ancient sea life. That's because the shale – a kind of rock made from clay – is in Yoho National Park, high up in the Rocky Mountains.

About 500 million years ago, the rock that makes up the Burgess Shale was part of a reef in a tropical sea. About 75 million years ago, when this part of the Rocky Mountains began to form, the rock shifted upwards.

The shale is special because the soft body parts of sea creatures were preserved here, providing scientists with information on prehistoric life.

The Burgess Shale contains the fossils of about 140 types of sea creatures.

Northern British Columbia

Northern B.C. is broken up by mountains, like the Skeena, Omineca and Cassiar ranges, and plateaus. Most of this region is sparsely populated, but its forests are home to wildlife such as moose, elk, bear, muskrat and beaver. On its mountain slopes live bighorn sheep and mountain goats.

B.C.'s northeast corner is a part of the Great Plains region, where there are foothills and large stretches of low, flat land.

About one-quarter of the world's bald eagles soar through B.C. skies.

Bears hunt for fish in **spawning rivers** during salmon season.

Quakes and avalanches

British Columbia has more earthquakes than anywhere else in Canada. About 1000 earthquakes are recorded each year, mainly in the west and southwest.

An avalanche is triggered when rain, wind, warming temperature or heavy snowfall loosens the snow on a mountainside. The snow hurtles down the slope in massive tonnes, burying everything in its path.

Bystanders witness an avalanche at Whistler. Thousands of avalanches, big and small, occur in B.C. each year. In winter, avalanche technicians are on constant watch and teams are trained in avalanche rescue.

Big B.C. facts

- Vancouver Island is North America's largest Pacific island.

- B.C.'s highest point is Mount Fairweather, at 4663 metres. Located on the border with Alaska, it is part of the St. Elias Mountains.

- British Columbia's population is over 4,380,000.

- About 18,068 square kilometres of B.C. are covered in lakes and rivers. This is about 25 per cent of Canada's total freshwater supply.

- Canada's tallest waterfall is 440-metre-high Della Falls, on Vancouver Island.

Della Falls

Chapter 2
Building a Province

Aboriginal peoples have lived in the west for thousands of years. Many different groups lived along the northwest coast, such as the Haida, Kwakwaka'wakw, Coast Salish and Nuu-chah-nulth. Food was plentiful here. Mussels and other shellfish, and whales and seals, were harvested from the sea.

On the southern mainland, Aboriginal peoples ate mostly salmon from the rivers. It was often dried for food throughout the year. They travelled from place to place hunting deer, bear, elk and duck.

In what is now northern B.C. lived groups such as the Tsimshian, Gitksan, Nisga'a and Dakelh-ne. They too moved with the seasons, following the animals they hunted.

Whose land is it?

Captain James Cook

In the mid 1700s Russian traders were bartering for furs with the Haida on Haida Gwaii. Far to the south, in what is now California, U.S., the Spanish were building an **empire**. When they learned that Russian traders were in the north, they set out to discover the B.C. coast for themselves.

Other Europeans vied for the same land. In 1778 British Commander James Cook sailed to what is now called Vancouver Island from the South Pacific. He anchored in a cove that he named after his ship, the HMS *Resolution*, and traded with the Mowachaht residents of Yuquot. When a record of this voyage was published in England, British traders and merchants took an interest in the area.

The Spanish set up a fort on Vancouver Island, where they captured two British trading ships. This angered the British, who threatened war. This event was called the Nootka Crisis. When it ended in the 1790s, the British had won the right to settle there.

Reached from two sides

In 1791 the British sent George Vancouver, via the Pacific route, to settle the Nootka Crisis and to map the area they had claimed. A year later, he sailed around Vancouver Island, proving that it was not part of the mainland. He then continued to explore and map the coasts.

George Vancouver

British Columbia's mountains halted explorers and settlers coming from the east. In 1793 explorer Alexander Mackenzie made the first overland voyage through the mountains. Mackenzie and his crew were working for a fur trading company called the North West Company. From Alberta, they crossed the Rockies, gradually canoeing and hiking their way to the Pacific coast.

North West Company explorer David Thompson followed the Columbia River, mapping the area through eastern B.C. and beyond, in 1806 and 1807.

B.C. became a valuable territory for rival fur trading companies.

The fur trade

B.C. was now open to the fur trade, which had started in the east in the 1600s. The Hudson's Bay Company (HBC) and the North West Company competed for territory and trading rights. Explorer David Thompson surveyed the mountains of B.C. for the North West Company.

Around the same time, Simon Fraser explored the land west of the Rockies. From Fort George on the Fraser River, furs were being shipped east to Montreal. But what the fur traders and explorers really wanted was a route farther west. This way, they could reach fur buyers in Asia and Europe more quickly. Fraser battled the rapids of the Fraser River and reached the coast in 1808, but without finding a suitable river for the fur trade.

The Hudson's Bay Company trading post at Fort St. John

A new colony

The Hudson's Bay Company claimed a fur trade **monopoly** in 1821 when it took over the North West Company. The HBC built forts along the coast and shipped furs across the Pacific Ocean.

At the same time, settlement of the American west was growing. The Americans wanted to knock the British Hudson's Bay Company out of the fur trade. The 1846 Oregon Treaty pushed the Company north of the **49th parallel** and it lost its headquarters at Fort Vancouver. A new site, Fort Victoria on Vancouver Island, was chosen by James Douglas as Hudson's Bay Company headquarters. When Vancouver Island became a British colony in 1849, Douglas was its first governor. He encouraged settlement and logging, fishing and mining industries.

Gold!

By 1858 the population of Victoria had grown to 700. When gold was discovered along the Fraser River, this number quickly rose. Thousands of gold seekers invaded the town on their way to the interior. Many came north from San Francisco, where gold had been discovered earlier. The gold rush forced the British government to make British Columbia a colony, to keep law and order. Two years later, gold was again discovered, this time in the Cariboo Mountains.

But few who came struck it rich. Many were not prepared for life in the B.C. wilderness and they gave up. Although the populations of both B.C. and Vancouver Island fell after the gold rush, the roads that had been built and the paths carved by the prospectors remained. In 1866 the colonies of British Columbia and Vancouver Island were united.

A miner uses a sluice box to separate gold-bearing rock in a stream.

Toward Confederation

In 1867 the Dominion of Canada was created in the east, joining together Nova Scotia, New Brunswick, Quebec and Ontario. This act was called Confederation.

B.C. was suffering from a huge road-building debt. The people of the colony were ruled by British government officials, and they feared the growing power and influence of the United States. Some people wanted to join the United States. Many settlers had come from there. Others wanted to join Canada or remain a British colony. In 1870 the Canadian government agreed to take over the province's debt and build a railway link to the rest of Canada. On July 20, 1871, B.C. became a province of Canada.

A coast-to-coast link

In 1881 the Canadian Pacific Railway (CPR) was formed to build the railway. Thousands of workers were needed. They came from all over, but especially from China and from the city of San Francisco in the U.S.

Workers toiled high up on mountain slopes and far down in deep gorges, building bridges and blasting their way through rock to lay railway ties. After the railway was completed on November 7, 1885, many Chinese immigrants made their home in B.C.

The province prospers

After the railway was built, B.C. began to grow and prosper. More people moved to the west, so there were more workers for its industries. Around 1890, many immigrants from Japan came to fish along the coasts.

Donald Smith hammers the last spike of the CPR's cross-country railway. Building it took five years and many workers' lives.

During the Great Depression of the 1930s, thousands of Canadians were out of work. Many rode the rails, and moved into shantytowns and relief camps around Vancouver, where the weather was mild.

By the early 1900s fish processing companies were being set up. The logging industry also attracted workers from Japan, Europe, China and India. Mining camps attracted settlers to the interior.

But the work was often poorly paid and dangerous. Workers held strikes to demand fair wages and better safety. Instead of listening to their demands, company owners hired replacement workers for less pay. Often, they were immigrants, which angered the workers even more.

Aboriginal land claims

When British Columbia joined Confederation, three out of four people were Aboriginal. As European settlement grew, they became a minority. They also began to lose their traditional way of life. In the late 1800s a few groups signed government agreements called **treaties**. The government assigned them to reserves, parcels of land set aside for their use. Many others had no recognized right to the land their ancestors had lived on for centuries.

In the 1960s and 1970s some Aboriginal groups were still fighting for recognition of their **land claims**. They held rallies, sit-ins and blockades. Today, these land claims are being settled in the courts.

During World War II, Japanese Canadians were forced from their homes with very few possessions.

Japanese internment camps

During **World War II**, Canada was at war with Germany and Japan. In 1942 B.C.'s 22,000 people of Japanese descent were forced to move to **internment camps** in the interior, or in other provinces. Even though they were Canadian citizens, many people in B.C. were afraid that they would aid the Japanese army in an attack on the coast. At the end of the war the prisoners were released, but they could not return to the lives they left behind because the government had sold their properties and belongings.

B.C. booms

British Columbia boomed after World
War II. New highways and roads were built
through the mountains. A fleet of ferries was
built to connect the mainland to the islands.
With improved transportation, B.C.'s goods
could be shipped all over the world. To
power the province, large-scale hydroelectric
dams were built across the raging rivers.
Vancouver swelled into a huge port city,
attracting people from all over the world.

Ferries make it easier to travel from B.C.'s islands to the mainland.

Chapter 3
A Wealth of Resources

While furs and fish originally drew people to B.C., its main industries today aren't just natural resources but services such as shipping and tourism.

Over twenty million tourists come to B.C. each year. Whistler, just north of Vancouver, is a popular spot for skiers.

A mining smelter refines metal ores in the Kootenay region of southeastern B.C.

Mining and energy

British Columbia's mountains are rich in coal and minerals such as copper, silver, gold and zinc. Of these, coal brings in the most money. British Columbia now has ten coal mines, located on Vancouver Island, in the Rocky Mountains and around the Peace River in the northeast.

Since the gold rushes of 1858 and 1860, mineral mining has been a part of the B.C. economy. Today this involves 30 different minerals.

Natural gas and oil are extracted in the northeast. Oil is pumped from below ground and sent through pipelines to refineries in Prince George, Vancouver, or the U.S. More than 2765 kilometres of oil and gas pipeline snake their way through the B.C. wilderness.

Timberrrr!

Over two-thirds of British Columbia is covered in forest and B.C. is Canada's largest exporter of lumber. Most of it goes to the United States for its housing construction industry. The harvested trees emerge from B.C. factories not only as lumber, but also as paper, furniture and chopsticks. Some communities began as logging camps, including Vancouver, the largest city in the province today.

In the past, loggers cut down giant trees using handsaws. Today the logging industry uses mostly machines, but unpaved logging roads into remote forests remain.

From the sea

Rivers that drain into the Pacific, especially the Skeena and Fraser, are rich in Pacific salmon – B.C.'s most valuable fish. Wild salmon live most of their lives in the ocean, but as adults they return to the place upriver where they were born. There they lay their eggs before they die. It is remarkable to see the "salmon run," as the fish swim upriver, jumping rocks and currents.

Not as many wild salmon are caught as in the past. Instead, salmon farming is on the rise. Fishers on the Pacific catch herring, halibut, cod and sole, as well as shellfish and oysters in great numbers. The fish are processed and canned in factories along the shore.

From B.C.'s ports, the province's natural resources and manufactured goods are shipped to the United States, Asia and Europe. The port of Vancouver is Canada's busiest.

The Okanagan Valley is one of five grape-growing regions in B.C. Most of the grapes are used to make wine at the province's many wineries.

From the land

Only about four per cent of the land in B.C. is suitable for farming. The main agricultural regions are the valleys in the south. Here, the rich soil is **irrigated** to grow fruits and vegetables. The Fraser Valley, near Vancouver, has the longest growing season in Canada. There are many dairy, flower, berry and vegetable farms here. Other important farming areas are the Okanagan, Similkameen and Kootenay valleys, where blueberries, apples, and **tender fruits** are grown. Most of the province's grain is harvested around the Peace River, in the northeast. Cattle ranches are found throughout the interior.

Hydroelectricity

B.C. has many lakes, rivers and waterfalls that cascade over huge mountain cliffs. The power of this rushing water is harnessed and used to create hydroelectric power. B.C. sells its extra hydroelectric power to the United States.

Most large hydroelectric stations are along the Columbia River in the east and the Peace River in the north. When dams are built across a river, the stored water floods the surrounding land, creating a reservoir. The W.A.C. Bennett Dam, on the Peace River, has created B.C.'s largest reservoir, Williston Lake.

That's entertainment

B.C. is a good place for stargazing. Not just high-in-the-sky stars, but also Hollywood film stars. That's because B.C. is the third most popular place in North America for making movies. Over 30,000 people work in the movie industry, mostly in and around Vancouver. There is also a thriving computer  graphics industry in Vancouver, where video games, movie special effects and animated films are created.

29

Chapter 4
B.C. Living

One in five British Columbians was born outside of the province, in other parts of Canada or elsewhere in the world – such as China, the Philippines, India or Taiwan. About 80 per cent of the B.C. population lives in the south, most of them in Vancouver or nearby. The city is growing as immigrants move into the area, as they have done throughout its history.

The high-rise buildings of Vancouver's downtown face the shore and Granville Island.

Vancouver's SkyTrain

Vancouver and Victoria

Greater Vancouver is nestled between the Coast and Cascade mountains and is home to half of the B.C. population. Year after year, Vancouver is ranked as one of the world's best cities to live in. It has a top-notch transportation system, including the elevated SkyTrain, as well as lots of green space and a mild, though rainy, climate.

Vancouver's Stanley Park, at 404 hectares, is North America's third-largest city park.

A mild climate and plenty of rain make Victoria green.

The capital city of Victoria is on Vancouver Island, reachable by ferry or plane. Much smaller and quieter than Vancouver, it celebrates its British heritage with traditional English architecture, shops, afternoon tea and activities such as lawn bowling. Victoria is known for its gardens, which bloom year-round.

The Butchart Gardens is famous for its flowers, fountains and statues. Over one million people visit the gardens each year.

The people of B.C.

B.C.'s residents come from a mix of backgrounds. Many people living in the province today have roots in the British Isles or parts of Europe, such as Germany, Ukraine or Holland. Almost ten per cent of the population has Chinese roots. Eight per cent of British Columbians have an Indian background. After English, the most commonly spoken languages are Chinese and Punjabi.

B.C.'s population is a multicultural mix.

Chinese New Year is celebrated each year in January or February. Huge parades with dragon and lion dancers fill the streets. Firecrackers are lit to scare off evil spirits.

Chinatowns

The first Chinatown in Canada was in Victoria, settled in 1858 during the gold rush. Chinatowns are areas in cities where Chinese immigrants gather to form a community. Here, Chinese-Canadians keep their heritage alive in their language, style of buildings, and food. Vancouver's Chinatown is now the second-largest in North America.

West Coast eats

Combine the influence of Asian immigrants and the local fish and produce of the B.C. climate and you get West Coast cuisine. This type of cooking is called fusion, or a mixing of different cultures. It features salmon, oysters, chutneys and berries as some of its main ingredients.

B.C. is known for its wild mushrooms. Wild pine mushrooms are picked each fall in the northwestern forests. They are shipped fresh to Japan or used by local chefs in fine restaurants. The fruits of the soapberry tree are harvested and used by some Aboriginal peoples in drinks and desserts.

Nanaimo bars, made with a graham crumb base, custard and chocolate, are thought to have originated in Nanaimo, on Vancouver Island, in the 1950s.

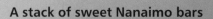

A stack of sweet Nanaimo bars

Chapter 5
Totem Poles and Potlatches

The totem poles of the Northwest Coast Aboriginal peoples stand tall and proud along the west coast of British Columbia. These towering wooden sculptures have become a symbol of the province, and are unique to the west coast.

Whale

Totem poles are carved from cedar trees. Figures called totems depict human or animal forms that represent a family's history. Common ones carved into the poles are the thunderbird, raven, eagle, bear, whale and wolf. These figures can tell the story of a past encounter with a supernatural animal spirit, or represent a family's clan, or group.

Eagle

A totem pole may be created to mark an important event, such as a birth, marriage or death in the family, or to honour a family's heritage. In the past, a ceremony called a potlatch took place during the setting up of a totem pole. At this event, which included a large feast,

A potlatch mask

the host would give away the wealth he had accumulated over the year. Sometimes dancers would perform, wearing masks carved in a similar style to the art on the totem pole.

Totem poles today

Present-day Aboriginal artists still carve totem poles. Many old and new totem poles now stand in public places in British Columbia, such as the Museum of Anthropology and the Vancouver International Airport.

Outside the Royal British Columbia Museum in Victoria is Thunderbird Park, where totem poles rise beside a replica of a Kwakwaka'wakw "big house." Nearby, summer visitors can watch poles come to life in the carving studio.

Thunderbird Park's first totem poles were erected in 1940. They were moved to the Royal British Columbia Museum to be preserved. New totem poles were set up in the park in 1992.

The Canadian government misunderstood potlatches and banned them from 1884 to 1951.

The oldest standing totem pole in B.C. is more than 120 years old. Called Hole-Through-the-Ice, it remains on its original site in the Gitksan village of Kitwancool in northwest B.C.

Emily Carr

Emily Carr was a B.C. artist whose work was greatly influenced by the province's Aboriginal peoples. She travelled to different communities on Vancouver Island and painted, in her unique style, the totem poles and the scenes from nature that she found there. She also wrote books about her life, including *Klee Wyck*, about time spent with the Nuu-chah-nulth.

Heina, painted in 1928, shows a Haida village on Maude Island in the Queen Charlotte Islands. It hangs in the National Gallery of Canada in Ottawa.

Chapter 6
Points of Pride

▶ Bill Reid (1920-1998) was a famous Haida artist. A picture of his sculpture *The Spirit of Haida Gwaii* is on the back of the Canadian twenty-dollar bill.

▶ Canada's first female prime minister, Kim Campbell (1947-), was born in Port Alberni, on Vancouver Island.

▶ The environmental group Greenpeace was started by a group of activists in Vancouver in 1971. Today Greenpeace has over two million supporters and is known throughout the world for its environmental campaigns.

▶ Rick Hansen (1957–) is a wheelchair athlete from Port Alberni who raised $26 million for spinal cord research on his Man in Motion tour around the world from 1985 to 1987.

▶ Cancer **amputee** Terry Fox (1958-1981) from Port Coquitlam inspired many people and raised millions for cancer research by attempting to run across Canada in his 1980 Marathon of Hope.

▶ Canada's oldest known tree is a 1300-year-old Douglas fir near Squamish, on the lower mainland.

▶ The world's largest species of octopus, scallop and sea star live in the ocean waters off the coast of B.C.

Glossary

49th parallel: The line of latitude that forms part of the border between Canada and the United States

amputee: A person who has had a limb removed

archipelago: A cluster or string of islands

empire: A group of territories or countries controlled by one country

fjords: Long, narrow and deep sea inlets surrounded by cliffs

internment camps: Detention areas in which Japanese Canadians were forcibly confined during World War II

irrigated: Supplied with water

land claims: Legal declarations of desired control over areas of property

monopoly: The exclusive control of trade

perilous: Full of risk or danger

spawning rivers: Rivers that fish swim up to lay or fertilize their eggs

temperate: Describes a climate that is mild or moderate

tender fruits: Fruits having a centre stone or pit, like peaches, plums, apricots and cherries

treaties: Legal agreements that guarantee rights to land and resources

uninhabited: Describes an area or place that is not occupied by humans

World War II: An international conflict (1939-1945) that spread throughout Europe, North Africa, southeast Asia and the western Pacific, and claimed an estimated 55 million lives